Fiddle Time Runners

Violin accompaniment book

Kathy and David Blackwell

Teacher's note

These duet parts are written to accompany the tunes in *Fiddle Time Runners*. They are an alternative to the piano accompaniments or audio tracks, and are not designed to be used with those items. These parts may be used with violins playing together with violas (using *Viola Time Runners* and playing the ensemble parts where appropriate); a separate viola duet book is available providing duet parts for all the additional tunes in *Viola Time Runners*.

We are grateful to Simon Stace for all his help in road-testing these duets.

Kathy and David Blackwell

OXFORD

UNIVERSITY PRESS

OXFORD
UNIVERSITY PRESS

Great Clarendon Street, Oxford OX2 6DP,
United Kingdom

Oxford University Press is a department of the University of Oxford.
It furthers the University's objective of excellence in research, scholarship,
and education by publishing worldwide. Oxford is a registered trade mark of
Oxford University Press in the UK and in certain other countries

ISBN: 978-0-19-356616-3

Cover illustration by Martin Remphry

Music and text origination by Katie Johnston and Julia Bovee
Printed in Great Britain

Contents

1. Start the show

KB & DB

2. Banyan tree

Jamaican folk tune

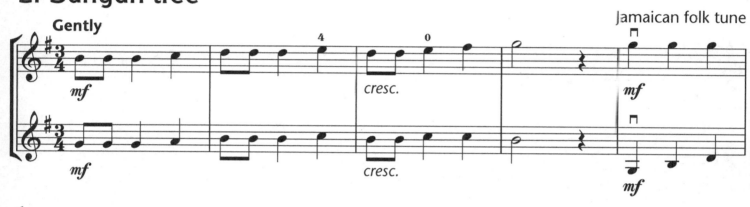

3. Heat haze

KB & DB

Relaxed

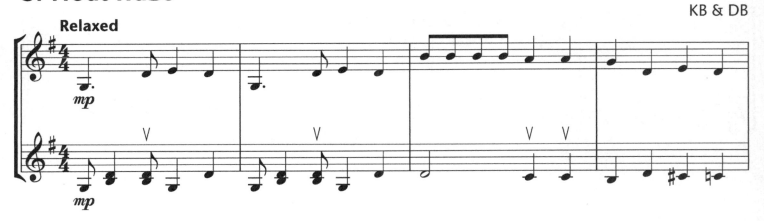

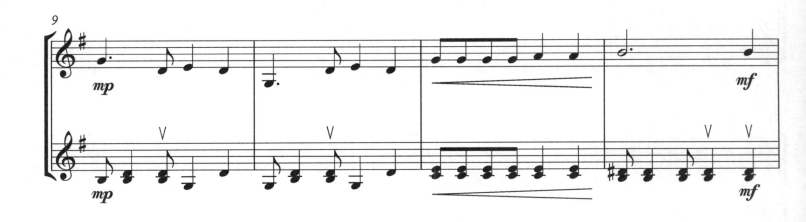

6

4. Medieval tale

KB & DB

Sadly

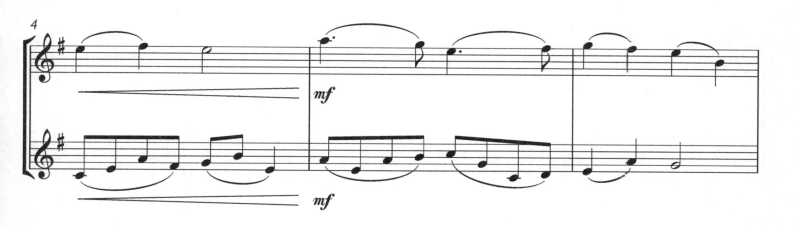

5. Cornish May song

Cornish folk tune

6. Chase in the dark

KB & DB

With menace

7. Merrily danced the Quaker's wife

Scottish folk tune

8. O leave your sheep

Gently

French folk tune

9. Jazzy Jingle bells

J. Pierpont

10. Allegretto in G

11. The Mallow fling

Irish folk tune

14

12. Noël

Daquin

13. Finale from the 'Water Music'

Handel

14. Ecossaise in G

Beethoven

15. Fiddle Time rag

Not too fast

18

16. Busy day

KB & DB

Busily

17. On the go!

KB & DB

18. Yodelling song

German folk tune

19. Takin' it easy: next page

20. Romani band

KB & DB

Fiery!

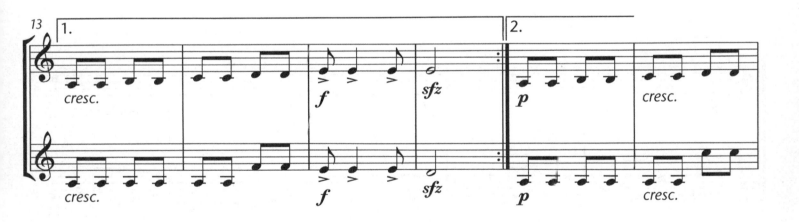

Nos. 19 and 20 are reversed to avoid a page turn.

19. Takin' it easy

KB & DB

Laid-back tempo

24

21. Ten thousand miles away: page 28

22. I got those fiddle blues

KB & DB

No. 21 is shown on page 28 to avoid a page turn in No. 22.

23. Air in G

J. C. Bach

21. Ten thousand miles away

With a good swing

Sea shanty

24. Prelude from 'Te Deum'

Charpentier

25. That's how it goes!

KB & DB

26. Hari coo coo

Indian lullaby

27. Summer evening

KB & DB

28. Flamenco dance

KB & DB

29. Adam in the garden

Jamaican folk tune

30. Somebody's knocking at your door

Spiritual

31. The old chariot

Sea shanty

32. Air

Handel

38

33. The wee cooper o' Fife

Scottish folk tune

34. Winter song

KB & DB

35. Rory O'More

Traditional Irish jig

36. Trick cyclist

KB & DB

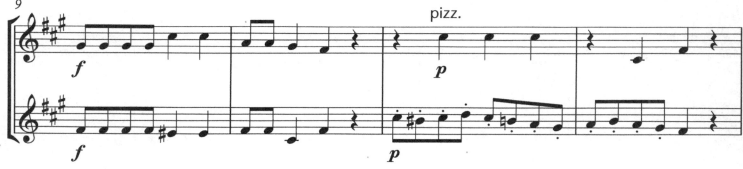

37. Aerobics!

KB & DB

38. Caribbean sunshine

KB & DB